Horse Mania
By Ed and Ruth Radlauer

AN ELK GROVE BOOK

 CHILDRENS PRESS, CHICAGO

Photo credits:
  Robin Radlauer, page 28
  Rolf Zillmer, cover

Library of Congress Cataloging in Publication Data

Radlauer, Edward.
  Horse mania.

  (Mania books)
  ''An Elk Grove book.''
  SUMMARY: Uses simple vocabulary to discuss
colors of horses, equipment, and clothes riders
wear.
  1. Horses—Juvenile literature. [1. Horses]
I. Radlauer, Ruth Shaw, joint author. II. Title.
SF302.R288   636.1   80-21550
ISBN 0-516-07784-8

1 2 3 4 5 6 7 8 9 10 11 12 13 14 15 R 87 86 85 84 83 82 81

A RADLAUER
Mania Book

CREATED FOR CHILDRENS PRESS BY
*RADLAUER PRODUCTIONS INCORPORATED

Horse mania?

Yes, it's horse mania.
Do you like a white horse?

You may like a white horse,
a brown horse—

—or a brown and white horse.

Yes, a brown and white
horse is nice—

—and so is a gray horse.
A gray horse?

Your horse needs reins.

Your horse needs reins
and a saddle.

Yes, your horse needs reins,
a saddle, and—

—some yellow hair.
A horse needs yellow hair?

Some horses like to race.

Some horses like to race
and some like to jump.

Do horses race or jump
on a trail?

A horse may jump over water
on a trail.

Take your horse
in a show.

In a show, your horse
may carry a flag.

When you ride in a show,
you may wear green.

When you ride, you
may wear dark pink.

You may wear dark pink,
green, or red and white.

Wear red and white?

Riders wear fancy clothes.

And horses wear fancy clothes.
A horse wears fancy clothes?

A baby horse is a foal.
It has to learn—

—to stand up.

A horse has to learn
to stand up and be friendly.

A horse has to learn
to stand up, be friendly,
and read.

Horses read?

Yes, it's horse mania.

Horse Words